Explorers & Exploration

The Travels of
Vasco da Gama

By Joanne Mattern
Illustrated by Patrick O'Brien

Steadwell Books

Raintree Steck-Vaughn Publishers

A Harcourt Company

Austin · New York
www.steck-vaughn.com

Published by Raintree Steck-Vaughn Publishers,
an imprint of Steck-Vaughn Company

Library of Congress Cataloging-in-Publication Data
Mattern, Joanne
    Vasco da Gama / by Joanne Mattern
        p. cm—(Explorers and exploration)
    Includes index.
    ISBN 0-7398-1490-7
        1. Gama, Vasco da, 1469-1524—Juvenile literature. 2. Explorers—Portugal—Biography—Juvenile literature. 3. Discoveries in geography—Portuguese—Juvenile literature. [1. Gama, Vasco da, 1469-1524. 2. Explorers. 3. Discoveries in geography.] I. Title. II. Series.

G286.G2 M38 2000
946.9'02'092—dc21   00-041312

Printed and bound in the United States of America
10 9 8 7 6 5 4 3 2 1 W 04 03 02 01

Produced by By George Productions, Inc.

Illustration Acknowledgments:
pp 5, 8, 10-11, 16-17, 38-39, North Wind Picture Archives; pp 14, 27, 35, The Mariners' Museum, Newport News, VA; pp 23, 28, 41, The New York Public Library.
All other artwork is by Patrick O'Brien.

Contents

A Taste for Adventure

The Age of Discovery began in the 1400s. They were an exciting time in Europe. During this time, people from the countries of Europe began to explore the world. Portugal, Spain, England, and other countries sent many groups of sailors on expeditions, or long trips, across the ocean. They were trying to find a sea route from Europe to the East Indies. The East Indies usually includes India, Indochina, and the islands off mainland Asia.

The East Indies were lands full of spices and other riches. The European countries were eager to trade their goods for these things. The country that found the quickest route to the East Indies would become rich and powerful.

A chart drawn near the end of the Age of Discovery. The chart shows Africa and Europe at the bottom and the Americas at the top.

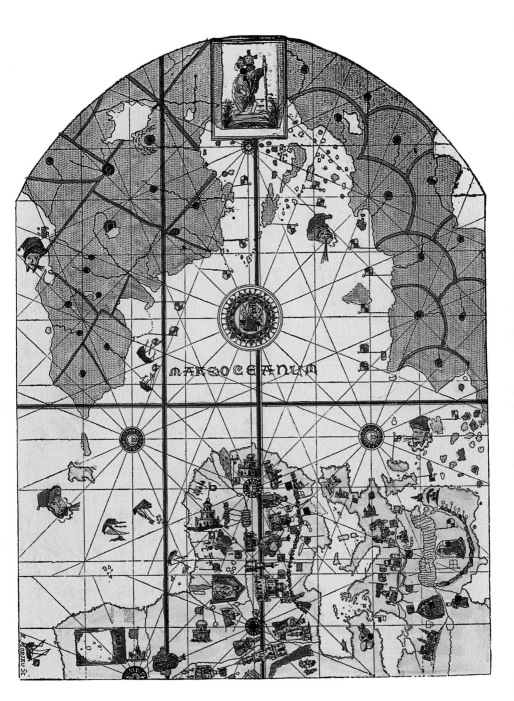

MARE OCEANUM

5

Explorers tried many routes to get there. Portugal's plan was to sail around Africa. In 1488, a Portuguese explorer named Bartolomeu Dias became the first European to sail around the southern tip of Africa. Because of the bad weather in that area, Dias named the tip of Africa the Cape of Storms. However, the Portuguese king, King John, thought that name was too gloomy. He decided to call the tip of Africa the Cape of Good Hope instead.

Once Dias sailed around the tip of Africa, he did not continue his journey. His crew was too afraid to sail into the unknown. Dias and his men returned to Portugal. The honor of discovering a sea route between Europe and the East Indies belongs to another explorer. That man was Vasco da Gama.

Vasco da Gama was born sometime around 1469, in Sines, a seaport in southern Portugal. Da Gama came from a noble family. Both of his grandfathers had been soldiers in the king's army. His father was a nobleman and a member of the king's court. He was also commander of the soldiers who guarded Sines.

Even as a child, Vasco wanted to be a sailor. Because he came from a noble family, he had the chance to go to school. Da Gama studied mathematics and navigation. These skills prepared him for a career at sea. Da Gama went to sea for the first time at the age of 15.

Along with most people in Portugal, Vasco da Gama was excited by Dias's trip. Over the next few years, da Gama made many trips down the coast of western Africa. Little is known about his early voyages. However, experts do know that he worked on ships that traded with the peoples who lived along the African coast.

Da Gama was a brave and very skillful sailor. By the time he was in his early twenties, he had become a sea captain himself. He worked for many merchants and soon became known for being a strict, fearless leader.

King John of Portugal

8 〰

East to the Indies

After Bartolomeu Dias returned, King John decided to send another expedition around Africa. But it took him a long time to organize it. For one thing, Portugal was short of funds. The country didn't have enough money to prepare for the expedition. For another, wars between Portugal and Spain broke out, which took even more money.

Also, it was hard to find sailors willing to go on such a long and dangerous journey into the unknown. Being a sailor in those days involved a lot of hard work. Sails had to be raised and lowered often, and kept in good condition. Ships were made of wood. Because wood is easily damaged by salt water, the ships had to be cared for and repaired often.

In the 15th century, it was dangerous
to sail across the seas to the Americas.

Along with the hard work came terrible dangers. Ships were often damaged or destroyed in fierce storms, and the sailors on board might drown. Or they might be shipwrecked in places where there was no food, or where enemies might lock them up or kill them. As well, their ships might drift for weeks on calm seas with no wind to fill the sails and move them along. Finally, accidents, sickness, and lack of food claimed many lives.

Almost ten years after Dias's voyage, King John finally ordered another journey. He chose Vasco da Gama to be the captain. Bartolomeu Dias would work with him to plan an expedition and design the ships.

Soon after he appointed da Gama as captain, King John died. Fortunately, Portugal's new king, Manuel, went ahead with King John's plans.

Of course, Bartolomeu Dias was disappointed that he was not chosen to lead the voyage around Africa. But he knew he had an important job to do on land. He and da Gama got along well. Together they designed ships that would be able to withstand the high winds and rough seas around the southern tip of Africa.

As they worked together, Dias gave da Gama an important piece of advice. He said to sail far out into the Atlantic Ocean rather than to sail along the western coast of Africa. Dias suggested this because the waters near Africa are very rough, and there isn't much wind there to push the ships along. Sailing away from the coast would make the journey longer in distance, but it would actually save time and make the trip easier.

Finally on July 8, 1497, Vasco da Gama left the harbor of Lisbon, Portugal. He was in charge of four ships—the *São Gabriel*, the *São Rafael*, the *Berrio*, and a supply ship.

Da Gama was the captain of the *São Gabriel*. His older brother, Paulo, was in command of the *São Rafael*. About 150 men made up the crew.

Soon after they left Lisbon, the ships sailed into a thick fog. Because the captains could not see one another, the ships became separated. Da Gama was prepared for this. Before they left Portugal, he had told other captains to stop at the Cape Verde Islands, off the coast of Africa, if the ships were separated.

By the end of July, the four ships were together again. After taking on fresh food and water, da Gama ordered his men to sail out into the ocean.

Da Gama took Dias's advice and stayed away from the coast of Africa. In fact, he sailed so far west into the Atlantic Ocean that, at one point, he was only 600 miles (965 km) away from South America. But da Gama knew what he was doing. In time, his ships picked up strong winds blowing east. Da Gama turned his ships back toward Africa and raced eastward.

On November 4, after 93 days at sea, a sailor on one of da Gama's ships spotted land. Three days later, the ships landed at St. Helena Bay in what is now South Africa. The crew spent about a week there while they cleaned and repaired their ships. On November 16, they set off for the southern tip of Africa, just 100 miles (160 km) away.

The weather around the Cape of Good Hope was stormy. Da Gama and his men had to sail against the wind while fighting huge waves and very strong currents. It took six days for the ships to sail around the Cape of Good Hope. Finally, on November 22, 1497, they rounded the tip. Three days later, the ships anchored at what is now called Mossel Bay, east of the Cape of Good Hope.

Da Gama's main ship, the *São Gabriel*

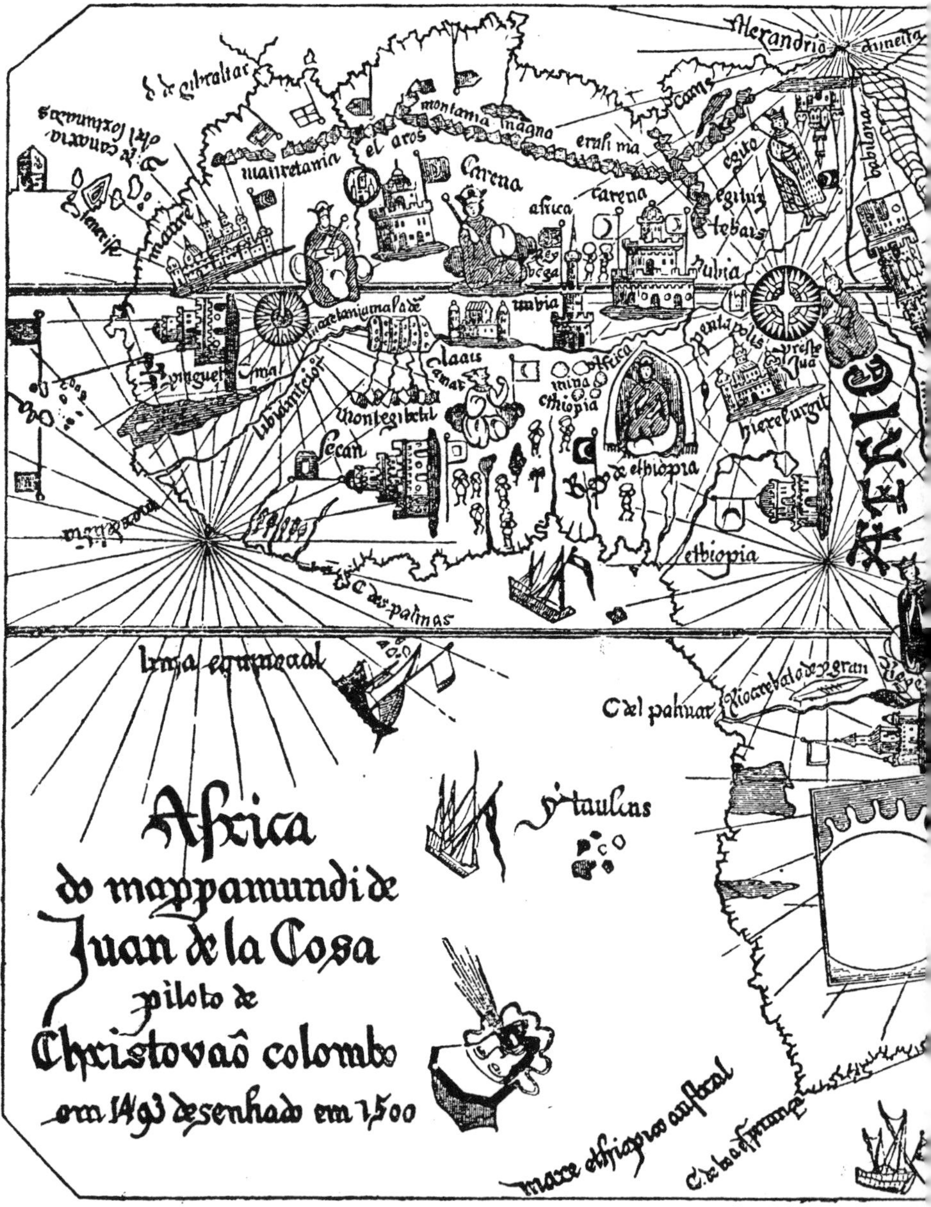

Africa
do mappamundi de
Juan de la Cosa
piloto de
Christovaô colombo
em 1493 desenhado em 1500
Alexandria
montania magna
mauretania
el aros
Carena
africa
carena
egito
tebais
nubia
ethiopia
ethiopia
C. des palmas
C del palmar

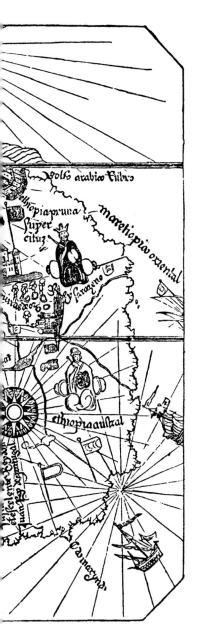

Da Gama went ashore and built a stone column to mark where he landed and to claim the land for the country of Portugal. Every explorer who sailed for Portugal followed the custom of building a stone column.

Map of Africa drawn by a Portuguese pilot who sailed there.

Trouble Ahead

During the journey around the Cape of Good Hope, da Gama's supply ship had been badly damaged in a storm. Da Gama ordered the ship to be broken up and abandoned. The supplies and crew from the ship were taken on board the other three ships.

As the Portuguese sailors rested in Mossel Bay, a group of African people came to greet them. The Africans held a great celebration, with dancing and feasting.

Da Gama and his men enjoyed the party, but da Gama did not trust these people. He wondered whether the feast might be used to cover up an attack on him and his crew.

Da Gama fired his ship's cannons to show how strong the Portuguese weapons were and to scare the Africans away. His plan worked, but it also made the people angry.

A stone column was built wherever a Portuguese explorer claimed land for his country.

As da Gama sailed away from Mossel Bay on December 7, the explorer watched the Africans angrily tear down the stone column he had built.

On December 10 the ships passed a stone column that had been put up by Bartolomeu Dias. Dias had told da Gama about this column, so da Gama knew this was as far as Dias had traveled. From now on, da Gama would be sailing in waters never seen by Europeans.

The ships sailed north, up the eastern coast of Africa. They stayed close to land. By this time, a terrible disease called scurvy had broken out among da Gama's crew. Scurvy is caused by a lack of fresh fruit and vegetables. It was a common illness among sailors until recent times. The crew's skin turned black, their teeth fell out, and they became too weak to work. Many crew members died.

Da Gama fired his ships' cannons, angering the Africans.

21

In January 1498 the ships landed at an African village. The people gave the sailors fresh fruit and water. Da Gama named this place Terra da Boa Gente, or "Land of the Good People," because of the friendly welcome and help they received there. Today, this area is part of Mozambique.

Da Gama and his men stayed at Terra da Boa Gente only long enough to regain their health and strength. Then they continued their journey up the coast.

On January 25 the ships reached the mouth of the Zambezi River. By this time, the fresh supplies had run out and the men were once again weak and sick. Da Gama landed, and he and his men spent a month resting and regaining their strength.

By late February, the explorers were on their way again. On March 2, they sailed into lands controlled by Arab traders. It was time to turn east and sail toward the East Indies. But first, da Gama needed to find a pilot who could guide his ships across the Arabian Sea. He invited the local ruler, or sultan, aboard the *São Gabriel*, to see if he could help.

Da Gama's meeting with the sultan did not go well. The Arabs did not trust these European travelers.

A portrait of Vasco da Gama

DŌ VASCO DA GAMA
VISOREI E COMDE

The Arabs had been trading with merchants in the East Indies for a long time and had become very rich. They worried that if they shared this trade with the Europeans, they would lose all of their money.

To make matters worse, the sultan was used to receiving valuable gifts from visitors. Da Gama did not know this, and he had only a few small things and pieces of clothing to give him. The sultan was very insulted. He refused to help da Gama find a pilot, and was angry as he left the ship.

Da Gama decided to show off his power and scare the Arabs into helping him. He fired his cannons, killing several Arabs. Then he took two local men prisoner and ordered them to serve as pilots. However, they were able to escape and return home. Da Gama and his ships left the area soon afterward.

In early April, the three ships sailed into the harbor of another Arab town, called Mombasa. The local sultan had heard about the trouble da Gama had caused. He decided to capture him. He invited da Gama's men to enter the city and get some fresh fruit and water. But da Gama knew that if he sailed into Mombasa's harbor, he would be trapped. Instead, he ordered his ships to anchor outside the city.

Later that night, two boatloads of Arabs rowed out to the *Berrio*. They started to cut the ship's sails and rigging.

An alarm was sounded before the Arabs could do too much damage. The crew of the *Berrio* drove them off, and da Gama left Mombasa the next day.

The ships continued up the coast of Africa for another 30 miles (48 km), until they came to the city of Malindi. The sultan there was an enemy of the sultan of Mombasa, so he welcomed da Gama and his crew.

Da Gama asked the sultan for a pilot who could guide his ships across the Arabian Sea. The sultan agreed and introduced da Gama to a man named Ibn Majid. He was thought to be the best pilot in the area. At last, da Gama had the person he needed to finish his journey.

On April 24, 1498, Vasco da Gama left Malindi. Ibn Majid guided the ships so well that after only 23 days they came in sight of India. On May 20, they sailed into the harbor of Calicut, an important seaport in southwestern India. Da Gama's ships were the first European vessels to reach India. The explorer had done just what he set out to do. He had reached the East Indies by sailing around the coast of Africa!

In the East Indies

Calicut was the most important trading center in southern India. Da Gama proudly erected a stone column to prove he was the first European to arrive there. Then he set off to meet Calicut's ruler and arrange a trade agreement with him. The people in the city greeted da Gama warmly. He thought that everything would turn out well.

At first, the meeting went smoothly. But once again, the Portuguese explorer ran into trouble. The Arab merchants did not trust da Gama. They also did not want to share their profitable business with anyone.

The ruler of Calicut wanted to keep up good relations with the Arab merchants. He also wanted to protect his people and his city. Therefore, he sided with the Arabs. He refused to sign a trade agreement with da Gama and ordered the Portuguese ships to leave the harbor.

Da Gama landing near Calicut, India

Vasquez de Gama
introduced to the
ZAMORIN (or KING) at
Calicut in India.

Then the people of Calicut turned against da Gama's men. As the sailors wandered around the city, they were attacked. Although da Gama had only a few spices and jewels to show for his efforts, he decided it was time to leave Calicut.

But da Gama's troubles continued. The ruler demanded that da Gama pay an extra fee for everything he was taking from the city. Da Gama refused. As his ships left Calicut on August 29, they were attacked by several boatloads of Arabs. Da Gama fired his cannons and sank several boats. Then he turned his ships west and headed toward home.

Vasco da Gama with Calicut's ruler

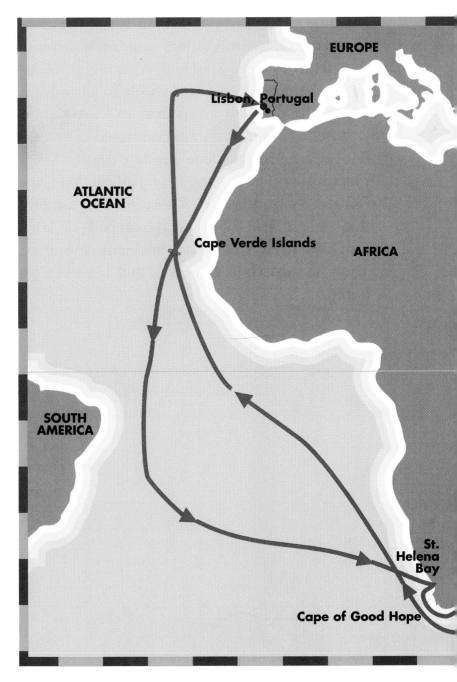

EUROPE

Lisbon, Portugal

ATLANTIC
OCEAN

Cape Verde Islands

AFRICA

SOUTH
AMERICA

St.
Helena
Bay

Cape of Good Hope

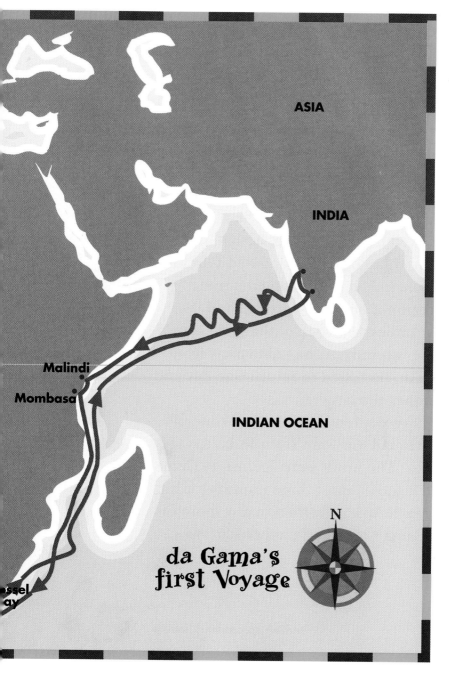

ASIA

INDIA

Malindi

Mombasa

INDIAN OCEAN

da Gama's
first Voyage

N

ssel
ay

Back to India

Da Gama was disappointed and angry about the treatment he had received in Calicut. Also, he had not done what Portugal's king had told him to do. He had not arranged a trade agreement between Portugal and the East Indies. Worse than that, da Gama's pride was hurt. As he sailed away from Calicut, he vowed to return one day and conquer the city.

Early September was a bad time of year to sail westward from India to Africa. The winds were against da Gama, and it took almost three months for him to reach Africa. By then, many more of da Gama's men had died of scurvy.

Indian spices and jewels

When he reached Malindi, da Gama did not have enough men to sail three ships, so he set the *São Rafael* on fire.

Da Gama reached Lisbon on September 9, 1499. Only 70 of the 150 crew members survived the 24,000-mile (38,600-km), 26-month journey. However, everyone realized what an amazing trip da Gama had made. He became a hero in Portugal. The king gave him a noble title and a generous income for the rest of his life.

In spite of his comfortable life, da Gama was eager to return to Calicut. He wanted to finish the job of bringing India under Portugal's control. But the long journey had weakened the explorer, and he needed time to recover.

Vasco da Gama and his men sailed the seas for 26 months.

Da Gama's Last Trip

In 1502, King Manuel named Vasco da Gama Admiral of India. Now, da Gama had his chance to return to the East Indies. The king sent da Gama to Calicut with 20 ships. Once he arrived in India, da Gama didn't waste any time showing his power. He anchored in Calicut's harbor and fired his cannons. Many buildings were destroyed and fires spread throughout the city.

Da Gama did not stay in Calicut. Instead, he traveled to the neighboring city of Cochin.

Calicut was destroyed by Vasco da Gama.

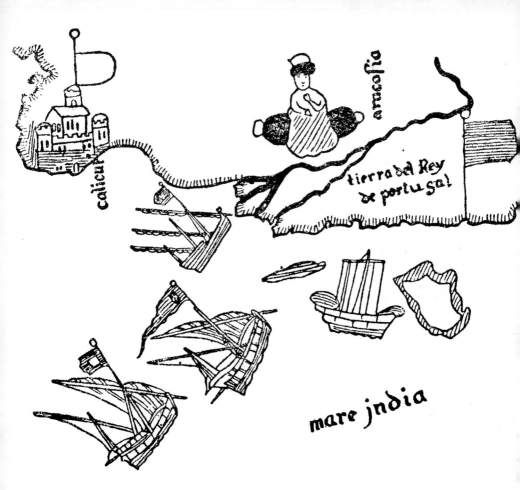

Calicut

aracofia

tierra del Rey de portugal

mare jndia

A map of Calicut and the south Indian coast, from about 1500

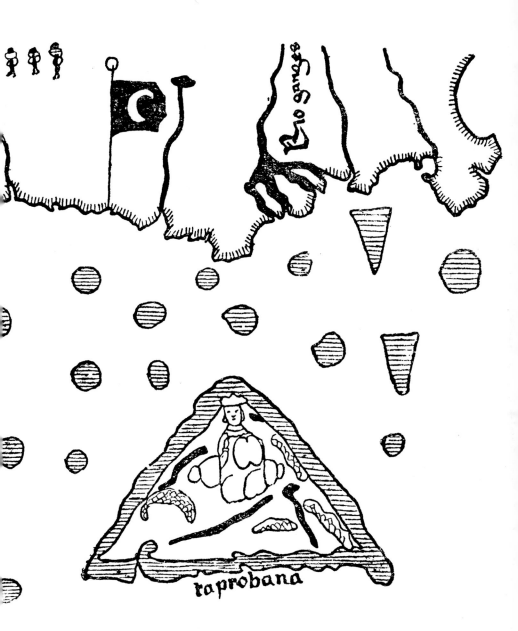

taprobana

The sultan of Cochin had heard about what happened in Calicut. He decided it would be better to have these Portuguese as friends than as enemies. So the sultan signed a trade agreement between India and Portugal.

When Vasco da Gama returned to Lisbon in 1503, his ships were filled with spices and other treasures. Once again, he was cheered as a hero who had done great things for Portugal.

Because da Gama had opened a trade route between Portugal and India, King Manuel announced that Vasco would receive a share of the profits of every trade voyage between the two countries. This made him one of the richest men in Portugal.

For the next 20 years, da Gama lived quietly in Portugal with his wife and six sons. In time, Portugal set up many trading posts in India. In fact, so many Portuguese trading posts were set up that eventually India came completely under Portugal's control. The king appointed a viceroy to rule India in his name.

King Manuel died in 1521. In 1524 the new king, John III, decided that the viceroy of India was not doing a good job. He asked Vasco da Gama to be the new viceroy.

Vasco da Gama opened a new trade route between Europe and the East Indies.

By this time da Gama was in his fifties. Although he did not want the job, he did not dare refuse the king's request. So he returned to India in September 1524.

Da Gama's final stay in India was a short one. He died after a short illness just three months later, on December 24, 1524. His body was brought back to Portugal and was buried in a marble tomb in a church in Lisbon.

Vasco da Gama was one of Europe's greatest explorers. His journey opened a new route from Europe to the East Indies. It allowed Portugal to control the spice route. This added to Portugal's position as a world power and led to it having an empire in the east. By bringing Portugal so much power, da Gama's journeys changed history.

Other Events of the 15th Century
(1401 – 1500)

During the time that Vasco da Gama was sailing, events were happening in other parts of the world. Some of these were:

1521   Hernán Cortés, a Spanish conquistador, conquers the Aztec Empire in Mexico.

1524   Giovanni da Verrazano, an Italian sailor, explores the coast of North America from North Carolina to Maine.

1534   Francisco Pizarro of Spain conquers the Inca Empire in Peru.

1571   Portuguese create colony in Angola, Africa.

1578   Moroccans destroy Portuguese power in northwest Africa.

Time Line

1469?	Vasco da Gama is born in Sines, Portugal.
1488	Portuguese explorer Bartolomeu Dias becomes the first European to sail around the Cape of Good Hope in Africa.
July 8, 1497	Da Gama's expedition to the East Indies leaves Lisbon, Portugal.
November 4, 1497	Da Gama lands at St. Helena Bay in present-day South Africa.
November 22, 1497	Da Gama sails around the Cape of Good Hope.
November 25, 1497	Da Gama anchors at Mossel Bay, east of the Cape of Good Hope.
December 10, 1497	Da Gama passes a stone column built by Dias and sails into uncharted waters.
March 2, 1498	Da Gama enters Arab-controlled lands in East Africa.
March-April, 1498	Da Gama visits Mombasa and Malindi to find a pilot to guide him across the Arabian Sea.

April 24, 1498	Da Gama leaves Malindi and heads toward India.
May 20, 1498	Da Gama enters Calicut, becoming the first European to reach India.
August 29, 1498	After failing to obtain a trade agreement, da Gama heads back to Portugal.
March 20, 1499	Da Gama sails back around the Cape of Good Hope.
September 9, 1499	Da Gama arrives in Lisbon.
1502	The king names da Gama Admiral of India.
1502	Da Gama returns to India, attacks Calicut, and signs a trade agreement with the city of Cochin.
1502	Da Gama returns to Lisbon.
1524	King John III of Portugal names da Gama Viceroy of India.
September 1524	Da Gama arrives back in India.
December 24, 1524	After a short illness, da Gama dies in India.

Glossary

Age of Discovery (dis-COV-uh-ree) The period from the 15th century through the 16th century, when many Europeans explored unknown waters and sailed around the world for the first time

Calicut (KAH-li-kut) A seaport in southern India that was an important trading center during da Gama's time

Cape of Good Hope The southern tip of Africa

Cochin (kow-CHIN) A city on the southwest coast of India

current (KUR-unt) A fast-moving stream flowing in one direction

East Indies (IN-deez) A name that once referred mainly to India but also included Indochina and many of the islands off the coast of mainland Asia

empire (EM-piur) A group of countries that have the same ruler

expedition (ek-spuh-DISH-uhn) A long journey for a special purpose

harbor (HAR-bur) A place where ships anchor or unload their cargo

Ibn Majid (IB-uhn mah-JEED) The native pilot who guided da Gama's ships across the Arabian Sea

Malabar (MAH-luh-bar) A region in southwestern India on the Arabian Sea

Malindi (mah-LIN-dee) A seaport on the eastern coast of Africa

merchant (MUR-chunt) Someone who sells goods for profit

Mombasa (mom-BAH-suh) A seaport on the eastern coast of Africa

Mossel Bay (MAH-sul) An African seaport east of the Cape of Good Hope

Mozambique (Mow-zum-BEEK) A present-day country in southeast Africa

navigation (nav-uh-GAY-shun) Using maps and instruments to sail a ship

pilot (PIE-lut) A sailor who sails a ship or boat

scurvy A disease caused by the lack of vitamin C

seaport (SEE-port) A city or town where ships can dock

Sines (SEE-nish) The seaport in southern Portugal where Vasco da Gama was born

sultan (SULT-uhn) The title given to a ruler in some Arab countries

trade agreement (uh-GREE-munt) An arrangement between two countries to trade goods with each other

viceroy (VYSE-roy) The leader of a country who rules for a king